D0504823

TOMMYINNIT SAYS

SAYS

THE QUOTE BOOK

First published in Great Britain in 2022 by

Quercus Editions Ltd
Carmelite House
50 Victoria Embankment
London EC4Y 0DZ

An Hachette UK company

QUERCUS

Copyright © 2022 Innit Inc

The moral right of Tom Simons to
be identified as the author of this work has been
asserted in accordance with the Copyright,
Designs and Patents Act, 1988.

All rights reserved. No part of this publication
may be reproduced or transmitted in any form
or by any means, electronic or mechanical,
including photocopy, recording, or any
information storage and retrieval system,
without permission in writing from the publisher.

A CIP catalogue record for this book is available
from the British Library

HB ISBN 978 1 52942 797 4
Ebook ISBN 978 1 52942 798 1

Every effort has been made to contact copyright holders.
However, the publishers will be glad to rectify in future
editions any inadvertent omissions brought to their attention.

Quercus Editions Ltd hereby exclude all liability to the extent
permitted by law for any errors or omissions in this book and for any loss,
damage or expense (whether direct or indirect) suffered by a
third party relying on any information contained in this book.

NOT OFFICIAL MINECRAFT PRODUCT.
NOT APPROVED BY OR ASSOCIATED WITH MOJANG.

10 9 8 7 6 5 4

Typeset by Julyan Bayes at us-now.com
Original illustrations by Julyan Bayes
Printed and bound in Great Britain by Clays Ltd, Elcograf S.p.A.

TOMMYINNIT SAYS

THE QUOTE BOOK

Wrote by **TommyInnit**
and Wilbur Soot

QUERCUS

This book is dedicated
to our friend Technoblade.

FOREWORD BY TOMMYINNIT

Among us. There, I said it.

Now, let's get to the nitty gritty. This is probably the best thing you'll ever read. I don't want to hear any of this *Harry Potter and the Philosopher's Stone* is better, the Bible, *Wuthering Heights*... all of these pale in comparison to this book in your hands. *Your* hands. I'm in your hands, dear reader.

Now, let's get to the nitty gritty. This book might not be a pleasant read for all, but it is a just one. I can say whatever I want in this. Power. Words are committed to paper forever. There will be a Wikipedia page on this book.

But still, let's get to the nitty gritty. I know some of you might read this on the toilet. That doesn't bother me, because we're close. I want you to read this and feel special, like I feel special all the time. You are special to me, dear reader. I love you.

I'm also a bit nervous for you. Some of the material in this book might offend you: that offends me. But let me tell you, it's going to be okay.

Anyway, let's get to the nitty gritty. Thank you for buying this. Unless you are in the bookshop, just flicking through this before putting it back on the shelf, in which case you are *stealing*.

Now... read this ... take it down... read now... sit down, read down. Time is money... get on with it.

But let's get to the nitty gritty. I actually have never read a book. I don't know what a foreword is.

There will be a Netflix adaptation of this. It will be worse. I will make sure of it.

The only person who can play me, is me. God, I look good.

Let's get down to the nitty gritty. I wonder if people in India are going to buy this. I hope so. I've always wanted to have my presence somewhere in India. India. In De Art. This is art.

If you've bought this, you're welcome. I'm about to change your life one word at a time. Unless, dear reader, you read books two words at a time, like me.

This has been my foreword. Now over to Wilbur. Wilbur, it's your time to shine.

FOREWORD BY WILBUR SOOT

Thanks for buying this.

PART I:

THE FUNNY. IT STRIKES

Who's got the mental skillet?

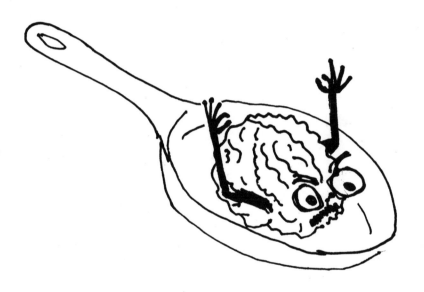

I could literally hand-throw a grenade into your bedroom window. And you'd die. And I shall?

I miss when I had other friends that weren't just you, Wilbur.

I put my balls in the dishwasher.

I don't want to go clubbing, I want to sit quietly with a loved one and read the Bible.

HOW WE MET

Wilbur on meeting Tommy

It was just before the pandemic quarantine. To fill the void of my days I decided to start a server for Minecraft content creators. On the launch day I had someone reach out and ask me if they could invite their friend. I said, 'Sure', and that's how I met Tommy. He was a nice kid, very nervous and insistent on joining, but he meant well. Aside from that it was a pretty bad day. Think I lost my phone on a walk.

Tommy on meeting Wilbur

It was a dark and stormy night. Or maybe it was sunny. I don't know, I have excelled beyond the need for weather. I knew today was the day I was to change an adult man's life. I got home, slammed the door. Mother asked if I wanted any curry. I let out a large, intimidating grunt, as I often do.

I logged onto Discord, ready to play on this new Minecraft server I had just joined. Another Minecraft server... (Sighs) *Sighs* in asterisks.

Then I got a ring from a new Discord contact. This surprised me. Usually I make the calls.

It was Wilbur Soot. Ah. Yes. I am familiar with his work. I looked at my busy schedule and thought, 'Yes, I have an ounce of time for him.' He pleaded with me to join his Minecraft server. Another Minecraft server... *Sighs*. I thought about it before arriving at the conclusion that I could use him. I wasn't awkward, I wasn't shy. I knew exactly what I needed to do: make a friend. I said to Wilbur, 'Yes. Yes.' He looked at me with his eyes. Except I could not see his eyes, it was on VC (Voice Chat). 'I will join your server on one condition.' I paused.

'What condition?' he asked.

I said to him, suddenly, 'Wilbur, you must never betray me. I have been betrayed before. It wasn't nice. The thing is, I always get my way.'

Wilbur, betwixt his desire to impress and his confusion, stuttered, 'T-Tommy, I will never betray you.' I looked between his eyes and said, 'Good luck, kid.'

Wilbur then told me how to get subscribers. I listened, half-heartedly, and then reached 11 million subscribers. I only ever use five per cent of my capabilities in respect to Wilbur Soot.

In conclusion: sure. I guess Wilbur is my friend. But at the end of the day, everyone is my friend.

Except baddies.

TOMMY & WILBUR'S WORLD

Hello again, sexy. It's me, Tommy. I have taken the liberty of detailing my brain (a successful brain) and Wilbur's brain (just a classic, terrible, s**t brain, no important thoughts, all in the colour grey) in order to make YOU, my slimy reader, more successful. You can thank me later, but I hope this helps give you clarity on what to think about.

I have done these diagrams in helpful charts because charts are always just helpful. Thank you, Frederick Chart.

A dodge in the moment.

Combat and abilities

Dodging

How can I charm more people?

My ability to parry.

This is how I avoid awkward situations and only partake in profitable ones. Dodging is a man's way of saying 'No'.

Charisma

Should we eat people

How much mud do I own at all times?

Why am I not getting my way?

Consumables

Oh, wait. I am.

Is it possible to eat man mud?

What if I manipulate myself?

Yup. Yup, no it is.

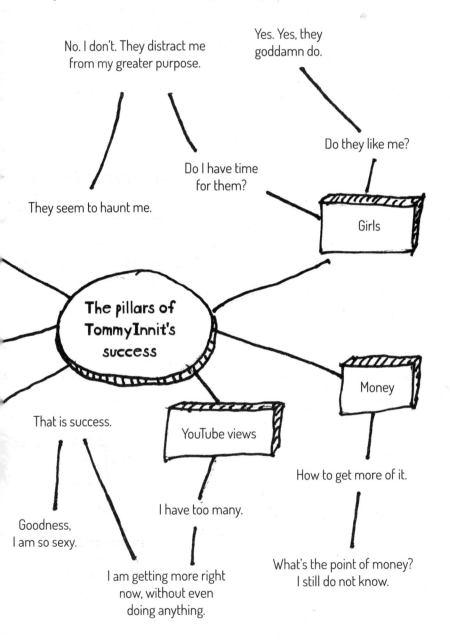

TommyInnit's brain (as wrote by TommyInnit, me, himself)

No. I don't. They distract me from my greater purpose.

Yes. Yes, they goddamn do.

Do they like me?

Do I have time for them?

They seem to haunt me.

Girls

The pillars of TommyInnit's success

Money

That is success.

YouTube views

Goodness, I am so sexy.

I have too many.

How to get more of it.

I am getting more right now, without even doing anything.

What's the point of money? I still do not know.

Wilbur Soot's brain (as wrote by TommyInnit)

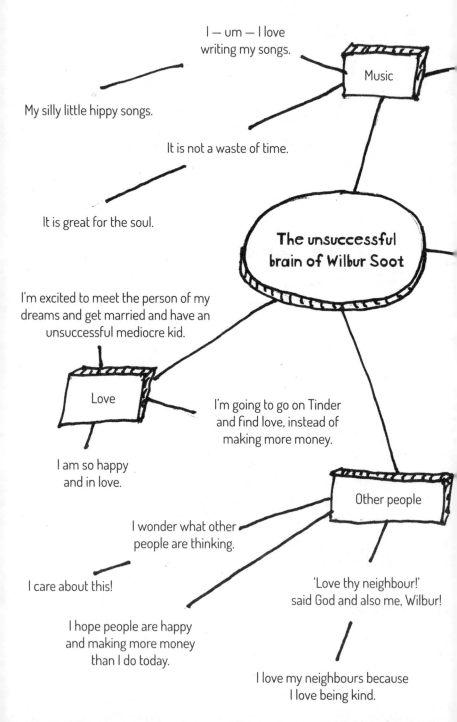

I — um — I love writing my songs.

My silly little hippy songs.

It is not a waste of time.

It is great for the soul.

Music

The unsuccessful brain of Wilbur Soot

I'm excited to meet the person of my dreams and get married and have an unsuccessful mediocre kid.

Love

I am so happy and in love.

I'm going to go on Tinder and find love, instead of making more money.

Other people

I wonder what other people are thinking.

I care about this!

I hope people are happy and making more money than I do today.

'Love thy neighbour!' said God and also me, Wilbur!

I love my neighbours because I love being kind.

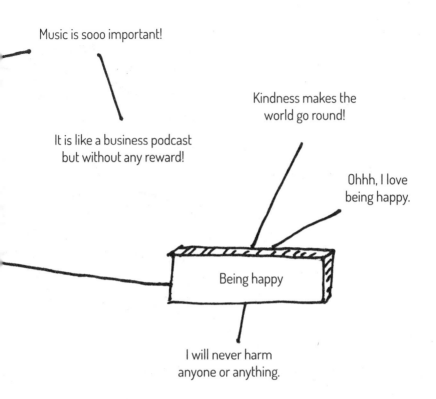

Music is sooo important!

It is like a business podcast but without any reward!

Kindness makes the world go round!

Ohhh, I love being happy.

Being happy

I will never harm anyone or anything.

Okay I feel sick from having had to analyse and subsequently demonstrate the inner workings of Wilbur's brain. If you ever find yourself thinking like he does, make a big goddamn change, chucko. I would rather die than be cringe.

Seriously, it is so important, my beloved listener, that you are successful! You should not waste your time with love and other people and so on. Please, listen to me, and follow in my footsteps, and you WILL end up like me.

If you ever struggle with anything ever, go back and read about my brain to get on track with what you should be thinking about. Get your priorities straight, kid. You'll die soon.

Love you, little reader

Absolutely all of this is wrong.

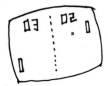

Well. Guess I'm a normal gamer.

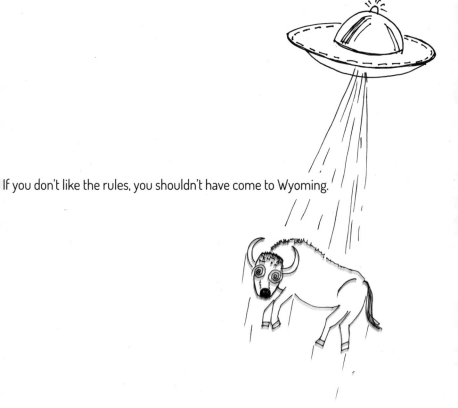

If you don't like the rules, you shouldn't have come to Wyoming.

Now I'm thinking of these nuts, everyone is in love but me, I've got a big telephone.

was panicking because Mercury was in retrograde but then Margerat Thatcher saved the day.

It feels weird calling my dad 'racey'.

I'm not ready to be a father, I'm not even circumcised.

She'd say you look good stealing from kid, stealing from kid, kid, stealing from any kid, stealing from kids.

Sometimes I look at my father's balls and I think, 'Hello, old friends.'

I don't want your hairy sushi.

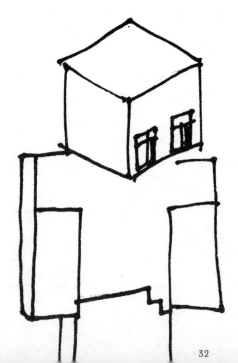

I think the world would be better if my balls were 80 per cent bigger.

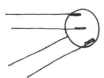

Tubbo

I once knew a man called Tubbo

He had a magnificent Grubbo

He was very wise

Which was no surprise

For all o'er land knew Tubbo.

But one day came the terrible storm

That wrecked and it wrought and it made all forlorn

Tubbo rose up, like a mighty… uh. Goddamn bee I dunno

Tubbo died in the storm is what I'm trying to put across here.

When I donate to charity, it goes directly
to funding Tubbo's satellite.

All Tubbo's streams need now is Viagra.

Phil, what would you do if I cuckolded you?

This photo is when me and Wilba first met. He was so happy to finally see me. He taught me what Cumin was.

I was so happy to meet Gogy. I'd heard the legends. The carvings. But he's a real boy. It just... it's these moments that make you. Y'know?

This is the day we first met in real life. My arms looked so big and muscly back then. Shame I had to shrink my body to make room for my brain. Still, a pleasant time at that. PS: Wilbur was really afraid to meet me, but I comforted him with my big hands.

Just for you

TOMMY'S VITAL FACTS

Medical Record	CONFIDENTIAL

Fact 1: (No... Number 1)

Number 1

[Tommy pauses for around 40 seconds]

Um ... no, don't write 'um', I'm trying to think.

[A further pause]

Fact 1

My... my eyes are baby blue, but they are big eyes. No, not doll eyes. Not deer eyes. They're not cute eyes. They're my eyes.

Most people find blue to be the colour of boys or intimidation, but I find it to be the colour of glory. Specifically in my head.

[Tommy leans back in his chair and stares at a wall]

OK. can we try this again? Please? Will, stop writing, start listening. YES? Ok.

Ahh. Vitality. It's the magic goo inside us that keeps us alive. Without it, we die. Or worse, become French. I shall not delay. Here, are my facts today (I'm so smart).

Fact 1

I haven't seen God. I've tried my best. I've looked for him far and wide, yet all I've found is money. Countless stacks of money.

Fact 2

I have an eight-foot vertical leap.

Fact 3

I am colour-blind too, you know. I'm putting this in the book now, so that when I make my colour-blind video in the future, I can hark back to this as proof that I am colour-blind. I just don't go on about it like some people.

Fact 4

I don't have a lot of friends.

Tommy, you tell me constantly that I'm your best friend.

I don't really need them. I have a lot of colleagues and I have a lot of lady friends, but there is a thin middle ground in which I am lacking.

Fact 5

My favourite flower. Ahh. I know you've been waiting to hear about this one, dear reader. A big one, asked by many people. Are you ready to hear the answer?

It's weaponry. Swords. Blades. Knives. I don't like flowers. Yeah. YEAH. YEAHHHH. Blades are the thin version of me. Knives. Can't live with 'em. Can't live without 'em.

Fact 6

I have no light fixtures in my home. I survive purely by echo location around my flat. I go out into my living room and make the most echoing sound I can think of, like, 'Tubbo.' I repeat this until I hear it echo back off my Marmite.

Fact 7

I eat purely for energy. There is no pleasure in food.

Fact 8

I use people.

Fact 9

I've never been manipulated. People have tried countless times. Some pretend to be the nice guy. Some flirt. I am completely incapable of being deceived.

Fact 10

[Redacted]

WILBUR'S VITAL FACTS

Tommy sent me this form and wanted me to fill in some facts about me. I'm flattered, truly, as I haven't had much to say in this book yet. I'm going to grab this opportunity and reveal all.

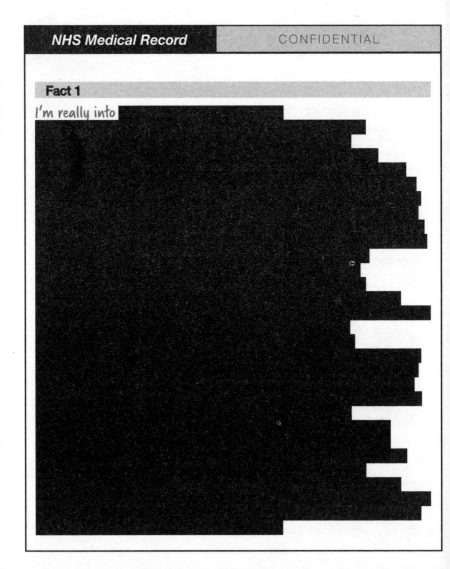

NHS Medical Record	CONFIDENTIAL

Fact 1

I'm really into

Fact 11

MY LOVE FOR WOMEN IS BEATEN ONLY BY MY LOVE FOR VIEWS.

Fact 12

THE DREAM SMP WAS ORIGINALLY CALLED 'THE TOMMYINNIT SMP' BUT DUE TO BRANDING CONSTRAINTS THE NAME WAS CHANGED TO ONE OF A LESS POPULAR CREATOR.

Fact 13

I LOVE BEER.

Fact 14

I TRY NOT TO BRAG ABOUT HOW I AM THE SMARTEST.

Fact 15

THERE'S A MILLION FACTS ABOUT ME, THERE ARE NOT A MILLION FACTS ABOUT YOU.

Fact 16

I AM IMMUNE TO DISEASE.

Fact 18

THERE IS NOTHING I'M SCARED OF. WRITE SOMETHING I'M SCARED OF IN THIS SPACE. _____

SEE? THERE'S NOTHING.

Fact 19

CARS REFUSE TO HIT ME.

TOMMYINNIT'S BIOGRAPHY,

Tommy was born sometime in the early 2000s. Not early enough to be actually affected by the horrors of terrorism unfolding here and in the US, but not late enough to avoid suffering the economic downturns that followed.

I do not envy him.

He grew up rich. His mother and father both pursued great career prospects allowing him a life unburdened by strife or financial woes. This is where the first problems arose.

Tommy's first job was a YouTuber. No, really, I'm not joking, the very first job he ever had was a YouTuber. I know, right? What the f**k is up with that? My man has never worked a day in his life.

Anyway, he created his first YouTube channel, Channelnutpig, probably around the time I was doing my taxes and he started uploading montage parodies, probably.

He pursued this pipe dream for a little while before deciding, rightfully, to switch his prospects to a channel entitled TommyInnit.

Now, for you Americans out there, the phrase 'innit' does not mean 'inside of it' or 'instead of it', it means 'isn't it?' Like the words 'ain't it'.

WRITTEN BY WILL

Tommy had his first big break as the plucky protagonist
on the HBO hit TV show, Dream SMP.
Here, he met such influential people as:

Tubbo

And many, many more.

There, he was scouted by the television agent Magelbus
Carmichael.

Carmichael took Tommy under his wing and, I remember this
day vividly, took him into his office and told him bluntly:

'Thomas,' (this was the style at the time), 'You need
to branch out into a more Minecraftless sphere. You
need to reach the upper echelons of YouTube content.
You need to VLOG.'

Carmichael, it's safe to say, changed Tommy's life forever.
Now, Tommy was shaking his ass for the Warner Brothers,
and posting TikToks left, right and centre.

Will there ever be an end to Tom's rampant flurry of
success? Probably.

A DAY IN THE LIFE OF TOMMYINNIT

I wake up, butt naked, arms stronger than yesterday.

> Tom has yet to make any progress in improving his upper body strength. Thankfully, I am unable to attest to if he was naked or not.

I pour myself a bowl of celery... cereals ... cornflakes ... the milk is golden, encrusted in gold. But not gold enough ... I slam it to the floor.

> Golden milk does not exist. Simply put, you cannot 'encrust' a liquid.

I check the vault. All is safe and sound. That means it's time for Minecraft.

> Tommy does not have a vault. He lives in a one-bedroom flat.

Suddenly, I boot up my hacked client. I'm the best in the game, they tell me.

> Tommy is definitely not considered one of the best at Minecraft. In terms of leaderboard ranking, Tommy falls into the 'unranked' area.

God, I love the people.

> Tommy has expressed on several occasions his dislike for the general public.

It's time for my morning sprint.

> I am very comfortable saying Tommy has never woken up in the morning, let alone sprinted.

I've never jogged. I either sprint or sit. I dash. Running with the sound (and the wind).

> Two very different speeds.

I can feel the people's eyes as they whip their heads around whispering 'There he is, the God boy.'

> Tommy's abilities do not extend to being omniscient.

I head to the jewellery store. There, I buy the jewellery store.

Then I burn it down (to prove a point, the point being that people don't need riches, material wealth, they just need spirit, my spirit. I often like to do philanthropic ventures like this).

> I do not think Tommy knows what philanthropy or jewellery are.

I enter a dialogue with a fit young man.

This has never happened.

He says, 'You're TommyInnit, aren't you?' I wink. He tries to kiss me, but I parry. He looks disappointed, but I thrive on disappointment.

Just simply not true.

I'm not the type of man who seeks validation from others, the only validation I need I get by looking in the mirror.

Tommy is the kind of person who seeks validation from others.

I go to the top of my building and snipe a few passersby.

Tommy does not possess a firearms licence or a firearm.

I grow tired of the hunt. 'It's almost time for bed,' I hear my internal body whisper.

What is an internal body?

I take one last look around England before I tuck my little toes into my big bed.

Comfy, I lie staring at the ceiling. That's right, ladies, I start to hex.

I literally do not know what this means.

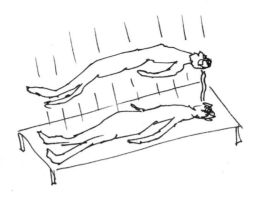

This is when I start to dream.

Sometimes my dreams come to me before I fall asleep. This is one of the many powers I possess.

Here, Tommy confuses headaches for dreams.

I start smelling a few odours from down the hall, but this only soothes me.

Tommy has a pyramid of Marmite in his kitchen. It sits directly in the sun. He seems to believe this monolith of biscuit spread's stench is some kind of message from the gods that he is right where he needs to be.

I feel my soul lift from my body as I curl up into another deep sleep.

A wonderful day for a wonderful boy.

Whatever.

To be continued...

I just want to swallow the big sea. All the octopi. They're so. They're me.

Stop doing music, Wilbur. You'll never be Shakespeare.
You'll never be Clive Rhythm. Just quit or let me take charge.

WILBUR'S BIOGRAPHY, WRITTEN BY TOMMYINNIT

Wilbur is sort of a music man, isn't he? He dances around like a little twerp.

But he's not a twerp, is he? He's a grown man.

Wilbur first started his career as a young man (as we all do) staring at the wall and knowing it was time to be a YouTuber.

But he wasn't to be just a YouTuber oh no, no, the fool had to keep going.

This is when he discovered a little activity some may call 'singing'.

Wilbur likes writing music, but writing music is easy. Lyrics are just YouTube titles, but easier. Just lots of little YouTube titles. I'd like if Mr Beast made a song. I'd cry to that.

Anyway.

As I was saying, Wilbur likes to write songs. This is so he can manipulate.

He tells me it's not, he tells me it's for the soul and for inspiration. It's not. It's for money, isn't it?

Wilbur, you clearly steal everything. Every word you write, every melody you hum, it's bad. It's horrible. Everyone else hates it, they just don't have the soul to tell you. I'm the one with the soul. Wilbur, I really think you need to reconsider. Your tall frame would make you an amazing basketballer. But you waste your time on music, melodies ... Music is stupid. Either watch with your eyes or... wait, no.

Music just isn't for everyone. Not everyone has the singing gene. You don't. Stop singing. You don't even wear jeans, you wear corduroy.

Seriously though, Wilbur, I think it's time for you to move on. This little scam of yours is over now. Move on. QUIT.

QUIT.

QUIT.

QUIT.

QUIT.

Wilbur's like, 'Ohhh, I'm gonna write a song ... about a girl ... and how she broke my heart ... ooooh. Then I wake up, ooooh it's time to release another single. But not before I put on my corduroy bottoms and jump up and down to maintain my muscular frame.'

I love the gym and heartbreak.

I'm a big bad kind of guy. I feel like I'm done.

That's Wilbur's biography. Tell him to f**k off.

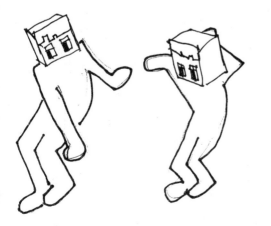

You're not allowed to go red-pilling on me again.

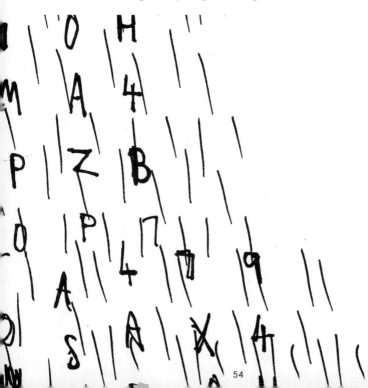

Just like in Civ 5, I have entered a golden era.

PART 2:
LIFE ADVICE
AND
INTERRUPTIONS

AN INTERRUPTION - WILBUR'S APOLOGY

I'd like to interrupt the creative flow and take a moment to apologize for things Tommy has said or allegedly done in the process of writing this book. I will address these as an itemized list for easier indexing and forgiveness:

1. Tommy's innate disregard for people's happiness

Tommy doesn't mean to be so blunt. It's just... he's never known any different. He is so young. So naïve. So stupid. One day, I hope he'll change.

2. His constant references to the Bible and to being God

Look, this isn't a non-secular book and I understand. And I believe religion is a topic that should be as openly mocked as the next thing, but Tommy may have gone a bit too far in letting everyone know that he is in fact God or that he ha fought/killed God. Please disregard this. Again, it's just his immaturity.

3. The cat incident

Now, I'm not here to say whether Tommy did or did not engage with that animal, but I would like to hereby apologize. He is a man swept up in excitement sometimes and his hubris can get the better of him. Please understand: he is not a bad man.

Please do not take any of his advice seriously, or to heart, or even really listen to it. I strongly advise just ignoring any of his words. If you don't, it will, most likely, result in your downfall.

Overall, Tommy is a good kid, but his extreme arrogance and lack of perspective result in him constantly, always, trying to destroy others.

You have been warned.

I want to enjoy throwing rocks in the sea, but I just can't stop thinking about my ex-girlfriend.

I show up like, 'Who's got the rocks, because I've got the tummy?'

A DAY IN THE LIFE OF TOMMYINNIT, CONTINUED

Please, God, no.

I wake up. This time I'm even more naked than before. That's right. I shed my skin again. Wilbur's just rung. He says that he and the band, they need me.

Please don't include me in your fantasies.

I stroll through the mean streets of Brighton, kicking crap as I go.

Brighton has a comparatively low crime rate for an urban area.

I swing open the doors of the Lovejoy (Wilbur's band) rehearsal. Their jaws drop and they go all wide-eyed.

Sounds painful.

Wilbur and co. scream 'Tommy! Tommy! You're here!'

I stare, blank-faced, nothing amuses me anymore. I have too much money to find joy in things.

'What is it now, Wilbur?' I moan.

'We need you to decide if this album is good. It's so important to me what you think. I love you.'

This is, yet again, completely untrue.

I cackle. Wilbur is such a dumb, stupid white cuck.

Well, okay, maybe a little.

I listen to the first note.

'It is bad. Start again.'

The band members wholeheartedly agree, nod their heads in unison and get back to work. Goddamn musicians. Ay-ay-ay.

I start heading back towards my home but see enemies on the horizon. I roll hard left and head into the colour shop to see if they've found any new colours for me.

What the hell is a colour shop?

My enemies find me. Joke's on them, I just discovered a new colour.

Tommy has the same prospective colours as everyone else.

They cry and weep as I overwhelm them with choice. I've already unlocked their minds.

I use my brain to get home. Safe and sound, I chop away the vines blocking my path and return to my humble abode.

These vines are most likely cobwebs due to Tommy's poor cleaning habits.

I flop into the great bean bag and let my thoughts run wild.

If only I could share them with you ... but alas, they are in another language I have invented.

Tommy doesn't know any other languages. He barely knows English — he asked me the other day what 'flustered' meant.

I do a little Comprehension, then head to bed.

Tomorrow the hunt begins.

Ominous. But at least it's over.

63

I took this at 5 a.m. when I showed up at Will's to write the book. He was so happy.

Will took this seconds after telling me he doesn't find me very funny. Or the last 800 words I wrote very funny. I've put them in the book anyway. Head to Tommy's Educational Segment and make your own decision!

This is my first pizza ever. Wilbur bought it me.

God, I look so good.

Philza Minecraft & Kristin
Obvious reasons.

This is Will at his band practice. I took this photo
without him even knowing I was in the studio.

This is us at dinner with Ash when I said, 'We should
make a book.' Wilbur took a Polaroid and we promised
to put it in the book if we ever did it. Hi Lol.

I think I'm about to hit rock bottom.

Hey everyone, prime now and you'll be entered into my talisman giveaway. You'll receive pride, shame and also talisman.

So basically, I think we're onto a bit of a girlboss here.

Phil, your kindness is a detriment. One day I will use you.

I ask my father how much my frosted flakes cost. If he says less than 500 grand, I throw it at a wall.

Sorry job, Tubbo's in town.

LIFE ADVICE FROM WILBUR
EDITED BY TOMMY

1. Stay true to yourself.

No. Sometimes you are bad. It's okay, it might happen. Try and stay a bit more true to me. Think to yourself, 'What would Tommy do in a similar situation?' If you do this more, you're probably along the right lines. You could occasionally afford to sprinkle a little bit of yourself in there but really, your personality should be exactly like mine. Hope that helps!

2. Do what you love — not what you're told to love.

If I did what I loved every day, I'd be a trillionaire instead of a billionaire. I would also be banned from several post offices. Definitely don't do what you're told. There are a few people superior to me out there: there's me, Obama and some others, in that order.

3. Create the environment that's right for you.

Ah, the digital age. It's all about creating. Have you thought of destroying? I often destroy other environments as everyone's gone soft. It's important every day to ask yourself, 'Have I destroyed something today?' Destroy things.

4. Choose your friends wisely.

Yup. But do you need friends? They take up time, they snot, they use your toilet. Consider cress. Cress tastes good, it's good for your physical wellbeing and it doesn't answer back. Cress will never backstab you. Cress will never say that you're not funny. Cress will never call you 'Timmy' as an insult. I have a garden full of it.

5. Develop positive habits.

What does this one even mean? Here's some advice: ignore Wilbur.

6. Create certainty and leave room for uncertainty.

NO! Create weapons, create defences for when the walls fall. You'll need them. There'll be lots of time for uncertainty when the looters arrive during the climate crisis and the apocalypse.

7. Be vulnerable.

Pffffffffffffttt. Laughing-Crying Emoji. L, M, A, O. I just lmao'd in real life. This is an absurd thing. Be hard. If anyone ever sees you crying, kill them.

8. Most things are not as bad as you think they are.

This is true. However, there are so many things out there that it's really hard to keep count. Are bees as bad as you think they are? What is global warming? Keep your head up, king, your crown is falling.

9. Be considerate of others.

Sentences dreamt up by the purely deranged.

10. View challenges as opportunities.

This is true! I am very socially opportunitied (this is a fact). It's yet another talent I was born with. There aren't many things that tend to challenge me. That's fine.

11. Trust your gut.

Your gut is just flesh and blood and gross stuff. Remove it and use only your mind.

12. Do what you love.

Do what I love: bank statements. Do my bank statements for me. Clean my house. I love house cleaning. See, Wilbur? It doesn't work.

Money only serves to tire me now.

I like ball theory.

Gasp! Wham??

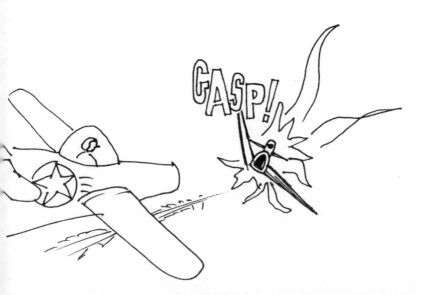

I'm thinking of preserving my wife in ice.

I'm so damn mindful I can see through the damn walls.

I love making people cry.

Egyptian goose but what's the point?

Will, if I ever get married, just shoot me.

WHAT I WOULD DO IN VARIOUS APOCALYPSES

Societal upheaval

I can make this stop upon uttering a single phrase. One in two people out of the womb are my sleeper agents. If you have no reaction to the word 'badminton', forget that I said that.

Mass global extinction

AHHHH! AHHHH! But then I would dodge it.

Geomagnetic reversal

This already happens to me, but I am simply too strong to be impacted.

(Wilbur, what is geomagnetic reversal?)

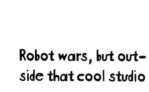

Y2K but today

Oh no! I would just jump through time again.

Robot wars, but outside that cool studio

First of all, robots can be tamed. Second of all, oh god. Robots. AAARGH! I would go to my garage and get out my big bluntener. This is a large, sandpaper-looking tool that de-amplifies metal. I would go around de-amplifying the scum-bots. Then I would change one button in their motherboards and BAM they all speak French. They all think in French. They all immediately sulk back to their *châteaux* and cry.

The sea decides it's had enough

Oh no! I must save the fishes. I go around with my great bucket and plop them all in it. I can't let the fish go extinct, not again. The fish may not look like it, but they are really cute and lovable and f█████████. I'd be like Noah in the hit TV show *Noah's Ark*, except I wouldn't have an ark and I wouldn't answer to some guy called God

I would get on my jet, with the fish (Noah's Jet) and we'd go to Amsterdam for a bit. There's no sea in Amsterdam, it's as inland as it gets. Also, this isn't really a disaster, but it's nice to have a silver lining: all the salt in the world would disappear, which is good because salt tastes bad.

Cars grow teeth

This one is genuinely scary because it could happen. I know they'd be after me because of all the things I've said about them when they weren't in the room. I'd find an electric car (not a car, just a computer with an ego), then I'd blend in with all the other cars.

Honestly, I'd drive around for a bit. I think I'd find it quite nice, the cars making a convincing argument about destroying humanity and chomp-chomping everyone with their big metal teeth. Hmmmm, maybe I could live like this. Maybe I could join the cars and settle down with my big truck husband and have many teeth-ridden car babies.

Slime people

I knew this day would come. There's really no defence against the slime people, they can go through doors, windows, vents (among us) and there's nothing we can do. But we can dodge them. We can hide in the shadows until the suction is done. It may be surprising to you, but I spent a lot time hiding from people during my school days. It'll be just like Bo Burnham's *Inside* but less sad and with more honour. It would be a real shame leaving everyone I loved and knew to get slimed but in all honesty, it's all about the survival of the fittest.

Meteor strike

I would scream and die.

IF I WAS GOD, WHAT WOULD I DO? WHAT WOULD I CHANGE?

First of all, I'd say 'Bye bye' to all insects. Those tiny scumbags just can't commit, can they? Either be a big tall animal or be dead.

They would be gone, poof. I am God, remember this.

I would make Tubbo much bigger. If you don't know who Tubbo is, don't worry, you will see him coming. I would make him the size of the Antarctic but sph- sphere- spjeirc- circular.

He will be my big beach ball and bob around the seven seas. He *will* be happy.

I will get rid of poverty, even if I have to kill every last child on earth. No matter what everyone says and how much everyone loves it. I think poverty is just not poggers.

I will get rid of taxes and then subsequently implement a new tax solely for me. Every person must lightly kiss a part of me without me knowing. It will be a joyous little game.

I will also collect an 80 per cent take on everyone's earnings, not including VAT.

I will then construct the palace. My palace. I will turn Paraguay (ahhh Paraguay) into my home. My home. My big golden palace. Once the great poverty war has concluded I shall lie there and rest. It will be made of gold, crystals and love.

REMOVE

Okay, now let's get a little more realistic, shall we?

I shall remove Denmark. Denmark has to perish. I will send them to fight the great Tub-Ball (a conflict from which they shall never return, or will be so psychologically traumatized that they are unable to resist me sinking their little peninsula).

I will also remove everyone's ability to imagine. Only I will be able to be creative. This means everyone will buy everything I put out.

Then I will give myself a million billion dollars.

This will satisfy me.

In return, as well as the current five senses, I will invent a new sense. Schrabö. Schrabö is the sense of knowing where every nearby pigeon is and in which direction it is currently travelling. While sensing Schrabö, you will also lose a sense of object permanence.

I will erase the past. We shall only look to the future.

I vanquished it all. I hope you pray to me every night. When you lie in bed at night, constantly aware of a new pigeon that has entered your proximity, you'll think of me. You'll OWE me. Because I, your God, have been here for you.

But now it is time to rest.

Ahhh ... Rest. I am resting.

Disclaimer: *clears throat* The publisher (frauds) have made me remind you that I am, in fact, not God. Despite what you might believe about me. I am in charge. But not in a spiritual way (apparently), just in a democratic way. If I was God though, I would ▉▉

ANOTHER INTERRUPTION – THIS TIME FROM TOMMYINNIT

I thought this would be a good moment to put a print-out of a photo here that would completely BLOW YOUR MINDS. I thought, 'What would be edgy? Out there? Unexpected?'

So I took a high-resolution image of my bum and submitted it to the publisher. I thought it would look great for the cover of this book. Long story short, due to my publishers' squeamishness, I've had to put it here instead.

Please ignore this page or, better yet, tear it out and bring it with you everywhere so that when you meet me, I can sign it.

Look, I'll even leave a space for signing.

See? Tear this book from your page and bring it to me.

Anyway, Tommy out. Let's continue the ha-has and pretend this never happened, shall we?

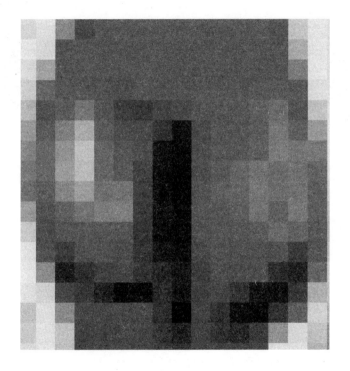

Sign here:

I have detected a lie. I'm like one of those dogs from *Up* that can talk.

I want to be the man that puts Tubbo out of a job.

You are simply not the noble Growlithe, while I am the s**t Zigzagoon.

No. No, Wilbur. You do want a girlfriend. I'm going down the chippy with a flyer.

Hey chat, I've gotta warn you, I am both controlling and manipulative.

Botswana, that's a type of car. No, wait, that's a Volkswagen.

I'm the Wayne Rooney of comedy.

I'm busy judging Ariana Grande.
Does she know she's fallen off?

I've got some moss in my mouth.

Venice, but the water level rises every ten years.

Hello, sadness, Wilbur Soot has introduced me to you.

I'm gonna die. In my mansion. Casey Neistat and Mr Beast will be there.
We'll all be crying.

Let's head straight to Slough with a lighter and a dream.

Hey Tubbo, incredible breasts.

I'm going to shag a wall.

God. Thank you for bringing me into this world. I won't let you down.

ONE LAST WORD OF ADVICE FROM TOMMYINNIT... ON LOVE

Simply put, love is not worth it. I've not had a bad experience, not at all. Just: love is cringe. It prevents you from achieving your longest held goals.

You want to know my story, kid? My love story? Okay, kid. Okay. Only because I love you.

I was betrayed. Cheated on. Stabbed in the heart with the knife of Carl Valentine. I was smiled at, and then subsequently not pursued. I waited. Oh, how I waited. But to no avail.

The thing is, you can't live your life waiting around. And love is a waiting man's game. Bad. It is made for pathological losers who don't care about money and do care about manipulating others lots and lots. Sex was invented by the government. Also, sex is bad and scary and awful. Practice abstinence.

At the end of the day, maybe... wait, here you go, here's a tip: just don't even go for it. Leave your love-y goals at the door and start grinding. Hard. Grind hard. And when you can look down at all the couples from your skyscraper mansion, you'll know you've done it. Just like me, kid.

It's time to level up. Get out of this place. Gear up, gumbo.

By Tommy. Inspired by Mr Beast.

PART 3:

TOMMY'S EDUCATIONAL SEGMENTS

Am I in *Groundhog Day*? Am I Charles GroundHog?

Stop spending time with women, start spending time time-travelling.

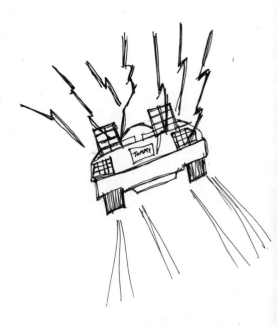

am so full of fury and bloodlust. I'm hunk, Wilbur.

What am I gonna do with a dead dog on my hands?

Why do I look so damn good?

Hey Corpse Husband, have you met Philza Minecraft?

Dogs got jim-jams on, Wilbur.

EDUCATIONAL SEGMENT: MATHS - THE LOST ART OF THE FOOLISH

If you have to learn about maths, you're stupid. People communicate through WORDS not NUMBERS.

Everyone has a goddamn calculator or a little punk-ass number boy by their side who will do their sums for them.

The fact that people choose to study numbers instead of something interesting like carpentry or dysentery astonishes me.

Sigh. (ah.) *ahhh* but yet, you've come here to learn. I'm not an ignorant man, I'm a teacher. So, I'll teach you maths, kid.

Buckle up.

It's about to get numbery.

MATHS IS JUST GRIM

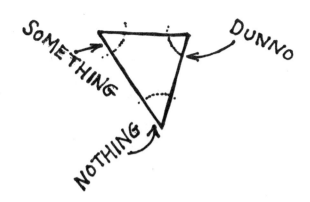

Maths fact 1

Maths can come in all different shapes and sizes. Uno (one), death, Pythagoras. All different types of maths and all different words.

Big numbers can sometimes be intimidating.

One of the things to know about maths is that it's all just triangles.

For some reason every mathematician goes nutty about triangles. Each goddamn corner has its own name. Seriously. Each corner.

The word 'hype' derives from the word 'hypotenuse' because of how goddamn giddy maths men are at one, especially the long side of a triangle.

They are a simple bunch.

Maths fact 2

Short people are better at maths.

Sorry, ladies, it's just the truth.

Maths fact 3

You can see maths anywhere in the world. How many paintings are there in the gallery? How many oceans are there? Which fish is strongest? How can I find this fish? Will he like me?

IT'S ALL MATHS!

Maths fact 5

Don't underestimate the power of numbers. They can be deceptive. Oh my, oh my, I've had my fair share of times when I've been deceived by maths. Maths can be manipulated. Numbers can stretch. Even money is maths. I think.

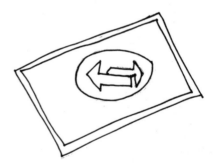

Maths fact 4

People who wear glasses unlock more numbers. It is to make them feel better.

Maths fact 6

Some numbers are completely misunderstood. Did you know one in ten people (this is a maths fact within a maths fact, baby) will pick seven over any other number? Why? It's not even that friendly.

The reason people pick seven...

Maths fact 7

The more you do maths, the more you will like it. It's like a drug.

Maths. It's simple, yet sturdy. It's the shovel in the shed of the learning garden. Maths is reliable, but it is not wanted.

Be careful with maths, kid. I don't want you going down.

My god. First of all, please stay in school. I cannot emphasize enough that this is NOT an educational book.
Secondly, I mean, I need to help Tommy. It makes no sense to me that he has lived by himself for seven months now. Seriously, what the hell?

No, Mr Beast! Stop giving your money away to people!
You need to keep some, Mr Beast! Please!

Stop being grumpy. I'm not going to talk to grumpy Wilbur.
I'm going to have another poo.

Nah, I think I'd be a pretty bad shark.

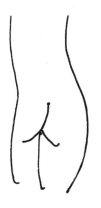

Gogy, your name is one letter from Orgy.
What does this mean for me?

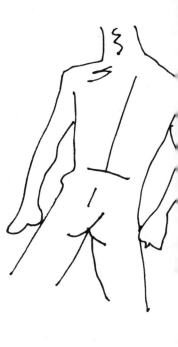

Hey Scott, why are you – uh – being mean?

Some people don't know what it means to wear a wolf coat.

We're not here to be friends, we're here to make money.

But what is witness protection?

I had my first kiss today, Wilbur, to the song 'The Winner Takes It All' by Abba.

I actually do not know how much I earn. What am I going to use money for?
Wipe my arse with it in public toilets? Yes! Yes! Amen! Amen!

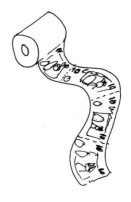

I say we make a pooing hall where we poo.

When I see an American and they don't find my content funny,
I think, 'I don't find your continent funny.'

EDUCATIONAL SEGMENT: SCIENCE – HONOUR AND GLORY

[AKA HOW TO DISSECT A FROG]

Instructions on how to dissect a frog

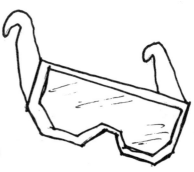

Warning: this isn't going to be pretty. You are going to grow up or die doing this.

Stop concentrating... no, I mean concentrate now... But concentrate on not vomiting.

You will need:

- A pencil. Go and get one now.

- Do not get a Bunsen burner. You make fire with your hands like God intended, or not at all.

- Goggles. Wiry substances made from substances that go round your eyes. They protect you from harm. They make you fearless. No one has ever attacked a man wearing goggles.

- Metal science ruler. It is the full-fat milk of the highly competitive ruler industry. Sharp. Sturdy. It's a goddamn masterpiece.

- Test tube. Mmmm, the long tubes that make up humanity. They're long, they're sturdy. They're loving. God, I love test tubes. But it's not about me, is it? It's about the frog.

Procedure:

Step 1

Throw the frog to the ground. Hard.

This is to splatter it.

Take note that its density is lowering. (A risk many scientists take is that it is too dense. I do not want the same fate to befall you.)

Step 2

Put on goggles. Now you are hard.

Step 3

Pick up the frog.

Insult the frog, e.g., 'You toad-hopping [insert appropriate swear word].'

The frog is now demoralized. The frog's density is lower.

Step 4

Get your metal science ruler. Start lightly, but dreadfully, chopping into your frog with the metal science ruler.

As I said, the goal of the procedure is to get the frog's heart.

What else will you sacrifice? Note this down: in order to avoid guilt there's one thing you must remember – frogs have no soul and therefore cannot gain entry into heaven.

Step 5

You should have started to get past the density layer and penetrated the frog.

Notice the frog has started to wriggle. Be careful if this happens, but do not be afraid. For you are the one with the goggles.

They do not make goggles in frog sizes. Note this down.

Step 6

Now I want you to close your eyes and reach out into the darkness. If you are a real scientist, the test tube should come to you.

If you succeed in this trying task, move onto Step 7.

Step 7

The frog's density should be so low that it is just skin. Stuff it in the test tube.

Now set it alight with the Bunsen burner.

If you do not have a Bunsen burner, you didn't follow your gut. You followed my ill-advised instructions. Scientists always follow their guts. You let me down, science kid.

Step 8

You should see the heart slowly float towards the top of your test tube. Flip the tube around like that cup challenge thing from... oh I dunno, the one from the Anna Kendrick movie or something like that.

Step 9

Lightly kiss the top which is now the bottom of the test tube.

This is the science seal. Note this down

Voilà! The frog should be gone!
With the heart still remaining.

Step 10

Now proceed to the volcano.

You've done well, little science child, but you shall go no further.

Cast the heart into the fiery pits of the volcano.

Do not delay. The brood mother hungers.

You are wasting time, science child. Get on with it. The brood mother hungers.

I shall not repeat again.

I shall not wait longer.

I shall not suffer fools kindly.

Step 11

Cast the heart into the cleansing fire.

Begin the ritual.

Cast the heart into the cleansing fire.

You should now be a minion of my unholy horde. Note this down.
Destroy the heart.

Destroy the heart.
Destroy the heart.
Destroy the heart.
Destroy the heart.

DESTROY THE HEART

DESTROY THE HEART

Conclusion:

At the end of the day, science is more than just a theory.

I know very little science is proven to be real. But I need you to trust your gut more; the world has gone soft and it's your job to make it hard again.

Live, Love, Discover.

This was your Tommy's science lesson.

Thanks for doing it.

Note to self: Tommy has become unhinged. Not psychopathic, not evil, just... moronic. I think it's time I have a conversation with him about this, honestly. I fear for how he'll get around the world, I really do.

ASSORTED FROG HEARTS
NEW RECIPE

My name is Philza. I am in control of the viewers.

I am actually very physically weak.

Let me out, I will get married in rage.

Oh Wilbur, my heart is a ten of ten.

Hello, son. Don't check my indirects, son.

Wilbur, you must remember, I am just a child.

She answered me! Pokimane answered me! I am now a man.

She didn't make eye contact with me once. That's why I like her.

I'm always loud to attract the opposite sex. I'm like a butterfly if it could talk.

There's only so many green up-arrows you can get before your heart becomes one big red down-arrow.

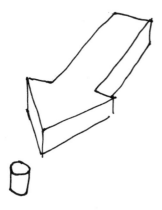

I know damn well what satisfies me.

Only people whose parents make over £200k a year know what a sausage fattener is.

I want to go slumming with a cricket bat.

did what Obama couldn't.

I don't care for fancams, I care for my primes.

God is dead and 7 ate him.

EDUCATIONAL SEGMENT: HISTORY & GEOGRAPHY— HOW THE WORLD WAS FORME

I know what you're wondering, dearest reader. I can sense it. You wanna know how this great, little... the big dome as we call it... How England was formed.

Luckily for you, I studied and subsequently failed GCSE History, so I think it's about time you listen up.

It was a quiet morning when the land came together. The god of the sea (Güncrapula) knew it was time to form it. Now, dear reader, many people tend to think of the Earth as a globe, but I need you to think of how it used to be: The Big Mouth.

Africa is the lips, Antarctica is the cheek, and so on in that fashion.

But the mouth was hitting puberty! A pimple appeared. But this, my beloved reader, was an unpoppable pimple. The yellow pus arose from the ground, thus creating the land of England. Alone stood one woman, Evelyn. Contrary to what the Bible says, there was one woman who formed the great pimple. Unfortunately for her, she was also the first to discover cholera. But her impact on the great pimple (England as we now call it) was long.

Then came the monarchy. They emerged, like we all do, from the dirt. Covered in sludge and slime, but also in a little bit of hope.

They built their castles in the North, South and left of England.

At this time, in the riddled dark ages, the middle of England was to be feared. Elders roamed the Midlands, fighting amongst such decrepit things as 'bricks' and 'gravel'. I'll get back to the Midlands again in a minute.

Up in the left, the Royal Family was blooming. Flowers blossomed, children cried (the happy kind of crying). This is how politics started.

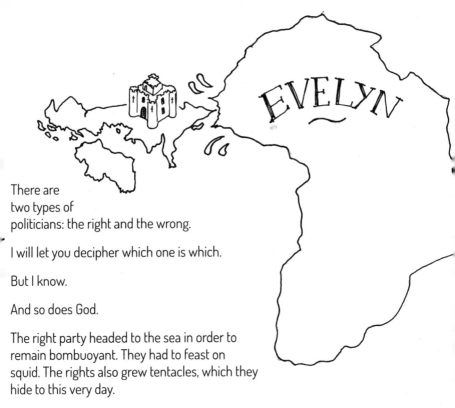

There are
two types of
politicians: the right and the wrong.

I will let you decipher which one is which.

But I know.

And so does God.

The right party headed to the sea in order to
remain bombuoyant. They had to feast on
squid. The rights also grew tentacles, which they
hide to this very day.

The wrong party helped everyone. Kissed them all on the lips. Helping them.
They do this to this very day in secret.

England's architectural structure is a core part of what makes England England.
The tall white building you will often see in photos is called the Kunkensribe. The
circular/prism-shaped building you will see often in London and Leeds is called
the Crystal Maze. The triangular-shaped pyramid you'll find in Egypt.

Not many buildings are rectangles, this is because of austerity.

At the end of the day, it's not about how we got here. It's about what we're going
to do and how we're going to do it. Plans change, sure, but history is written
down. I've just been tasked as the boy to recall it.

I hope you've learned from this... No. You have learned from this.

Recite this to others.

Like the Bible.

Scott. Remember this. Right. Remember this. For the rest of your life. Just. Stop. Grow up.

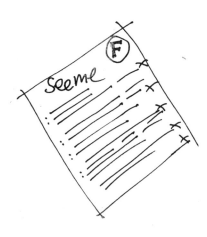

You're putting me in the quote book, but I'm stood right here.
It's like parents' evening all over again.

The quote book is a gift of life, just like hearing and death.

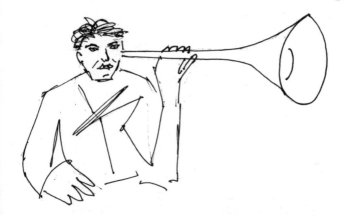

If only I'd brought my vlog knife.

TOMMY'S LOVE POETRY

Important note: I came across these poems on Tommy's desk. I asked him if I could put them in the book and he said, 'Good luck, kid.' I guess that means yes? I don't f***king know anymore.

Poem 1

The heart, it pulps.

It bumps.

It bounces.

But it still loves?

My heart is full of blood.

It sends it to my brain so I can think of you.

And it sends it to my bbbbbbbbbbbbbbbbb

Balls. We all have them. We all love them.

I didn't just love her for her balls.

Poem 2

Love flows through the air, it truly does. But you can't breathe it. No,
no no. No. No, you can't breathe love. No. Don't try to breathe love. NO.
No, no no, no, no no no. NO, it's bloody. NO, no, no no no no no no.

If love is the ocean, then fish are...

I once had a girlfriend. She was like seaweed; she hated when I looked at her.

You will fall out of love, I will laugh. Every time a couple breaks up, I grow stronger.

I thrive on loss. Attention too. But mainly loss.

Sometimes I cause natural disasters. I once rearranged
a woman with my love tsunami.

Poem 3

Loss, *sighs* (but the big kind of sigh)

I've lost things people, dogs, spells

But at the end of it all I'm still the same man

And so are you.

No matter what you're going through it's going to be okay.

It'll pass. And even if you never get used to that hole in your heart, it'll get easier

And that love you held for the person you lost will never go.

However.

I am better than you

And the person you lost

Never forget that

Buy my books.

Poem 4

France is like a box of chocolates

I want to throw it out

Whenever I think of France my whole body starts to pout

I hate France

I hate France

I hate France

I hate France

If you're from France you should really reconsider

Why live in this place that is so bitter?

If you are from France you have no life, no love, no home

Even the walls are bad in France

How do you make walls bad?

We don't love you, France

Word on the street is, watch your back

It won't be long until a Tommy attack

Amen.

Sigh. I've sighed a lot assisting in the writing process of this book. Tommy's a good kid. I promise. But, like the noble llama, he spits too hard. It's important you remember that he is a moron.

It's not that I don't like him, I love the kid, it's just I hate him.

I'm sorry for what he says. He is a dumb-ass.

Please never show your parents this book.

I think I'm more of a female lion myself.

But, God, what I wouldn't do to live in Wyoming.

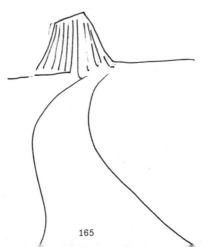

No. No. I'm not a little beach coma.

We're really just chilling, fellas.

Let's get rid of the fur boy.

Good news: I got you a woman. Bad news: she's American.

Good
Wife
GUIDE

How can I study the YouTube algorithm if there's a woman in my home?

I took one day off the algorithm to study women.

Dave. Man's got shot.

I'm a man of many men.

I'm streaming, Mum! Yes, I know the space station is cool, Mum, but I'm in a Minecraft tournament! Oh that's poggers, Mum!

I don't have crushes on women, they have crushes on me. Even if I did, I have to hide them for my brand. I must stay womanless or keep them in the shadows.

It's steak and chips night, gents. I'm going to beef up for Vikkstar.

Wilbur, can you stop telling these children about the futility of life on Minecraft Hypixel and how they're all going to die?

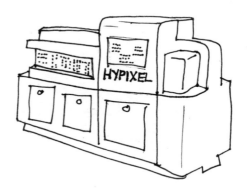

Things that
be Crazy:

Turtles

Loved ones

Ladies

I was planning it out in my stress dream, Will. I plan a lot of things about you in my stress dream.

In LA I just say things that make me seem more interesting. They say, 'I just bought a Lamborghini', I say, 'I've just buried my dad.'

I'm going to go slumming.

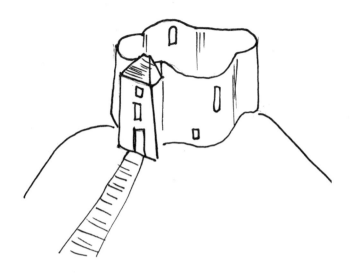

Let me take you to York, baby, on a Minecraft-building inspiration trip.

I watched his *Tribute to Minecraft* and cried, now I have to show him pictures of my girlfriend.

HELLO DARK TIMES

I'll carry your baby.

I'm going to make a website called, 'I'll listen if you want to cry'.

I made a cake for my dad. I just put a tin on his head, poured butter into his mouth and lit him on fire.

I've always wanted to be a mirror.

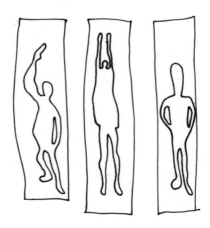

I'll help you, Phil, I want your wife and money.

A CONVERSATION WHERE WILL TRIES TO REASON WITH TOM

Hello Tommy.

> Hello Wilbur.

It's nice to have you here.

> Yup. It is.

You alright?

> I'm better than you have ever been, will ever be or were.
> I am lightning. I am God. Thunder: it's in my blood.

Why do you think I've brought you here today?

> I think you wanna pick my brain. My glorious sexy brain. I've
> noticed, no, I've observed you (and the rest) are falling off.
> You want my input, don't you? Well, it won't be free.

Tommy, your friends and I are worried about you.

That frog experiment...

I've got eyes like a bat, Wilbur.
I can see f***ing everything.

I know what's going on here.
'Worried.' WORRIED?

The only thing you should
be worried about is how
irresistible I am to women. I'm
irresistible to all of them. ALL OF THEM. They're all waiting for me
to get home so they can say things in italics like, 'Hi, Tommy!'

You've been spending so much time on your own lately ... we
just wanted to make sure you were doing okay?

Wilbur. Wilbur. First of all, when I talk it is to be heard. When you listen
you are to be wooed. This is not my intention, this is just how it goes.

Second of all, I'm not really alone, am I? First of all,
the presence of God is always with me.

Third of all, I'm always absorbing. I am the sponge
after all. The big wet soggy cloth of knowledge.

I feel like I'm not getting through to you.

Well, fine. Fine. Do you want me to listen to you? Time is money
and YOU booked this in MY digital calendar. You have another
eight-and-a-half minutes so PLEASE, try your hardest.

Okay, I feel like writing this book is giving you feelings of
grandeur. I think you need to take a step back and really
consider what you're doing here.

I don't know what any of that means.

I think, Tommy, you need to calm down.

Do you know how much money I have? How
much money? So much. So, so much.

I cannot calm down, for I am speed. I'm Batman. I'm running
a race that no one else can win. I am at the front of the pack.
I am the wolf, you are the dirt I tread on. One day someone

will try to plant a flower in you and I will stand in it.

'Bye bye, pretty little flower,' I'll think. Before you'll return to mud. The rain will drain you into the great river. Enjoy it while it lasts, kid.

I am the great canine.

When was the last time you spoke to a person who wasn't me?

Define 'person'?

A person is a human being. I want to know who you have spoken to recently, outside of me and yourself?

Sighs in relief People. They're tiring, you know. The reason I only speak to you, Wilbur, is I know you'll die without me. You're like a dog on a leash and as soon as I let you off you'll jump off a cliff. I have to keep you tethered.

You see, I am the humble dog walker. I drive my glorious van around the neighbourhood and I steal the dogs. The dog walker does not have time for other people, let alone other dogs. Whenever I am lost on what to do I just think to myself, 'How many oranges will be in my fruit bowl of life?'

To me, Wilbur, you are the strange inedible bit atop a pear. I am the citrus of the orange. Yet I also hold the bowl.

My hands are strong. My brain is chalked full of wisdom.

Wilbur. William. Can I call you William? I'll be calling you William henceforth, sir.

I don't have a lot of friends. You are the one I choose to speak to.

Okay?

At the end of the day, we're all going to die. I just know that my legacy and my Wikipedia page... my... my legacy is going to be long.

This is hopeless.

Yup. My brain is unintelligible to those with under 30 million followers.

Eight and a half minutes of silence pass

I really... Uhm... I really... I take back what I said. Wilbur, if you're going to any parties soon, please invite me.

okay, Tommy.

Thanks, Wilbur.

I've got a stomach full of battery acid and a creative mind.

I'll have a fist full of sh*t for you and a gob full of milk for me.

I'm going to Shoreditch to get a salad in my vagina.

I don't have time to make memes, I've got to make children.

I've got some great tits.

Maybe our Prime Minister really is a cuck.

Tubbo, what are your biggest turn-ons?

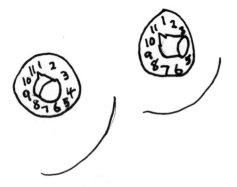

In my belly live three big spiders.

Hey guys. Tommy here. You remember me? It's the end of my book so I would like give thanks. I will be dividing these into 'soft thanks' and 'hard thanks'. If you are of a solemn disposition, please do not read the hard thanks. If you are a big, tough man, please do not read the soft thanks.

I shall dispense my gratitude now...

Soft thanks

I'd like to thank **God** for bringing me into the world. Ahhh, thank you God. (This is me praying). I'd like to thank **Tubbo** for keeping me soft and also staying out of my way while I write this. I'm always plush around Tubbo. It means the world to me. Soft thanks to **Wilbur** for writing down the words what I say. I'm sure many of the prophets will be doing it in years to come. But for you to be the first prophet... What is a prophet? But for you to be the first man to write down my scribbles, it really means a lot, big bro. Soft thanks to **Phil**, my e-dad. He always gives me e-advice like 'Don't tweet photos of your balls, son', 'Be good' and 'Wish for others as you would wish for yourself' – but no-one could handle what I wish for myself. Thank you to **Imagination**. Without you, I wouldn't be able to have my little mind-box. Thank you to the **five senses**. Especially **Touch**. Wait, no... thank you to **Hearing**. Thank you, Hearing. Very cool. Thank you to **Minecraft** for letting me rise above you. And thanks to all the **hills**, and other **big things** that give me perspective. Thanks to the **sea** for not sucking me up. I am deathly afraid of you. Thank you to **octopi**, you creepy but lovable scum. **Toads**, I see you. **Wind resistance...** You hold me back when I need it most, such as when I am trying (as I often do) to surpass terminal velocity. **Agriculture**, keep those crazy girlies fed. **Pottery**! How else would things be made out of clay? The **rainbow**. **Freedom** and/or **cones**. And the biggest thank you of all, to me, **Tommy**. And all other mes that may exist.

Soft all the way to the bottom

Hard thanks

Listen up, guys. Thanks to **swords**. Like batons but wicked sick. Thanks to **chillies**. But more importantly **ginger**. Ginger keeps sh*t HOT. Thanks to the colour **red** (keeps sh*t b*tchin'). Thanks to **Tubbo**. He keeps me strong. Thanks to the **law**, reminding me of my limits. Hard thanks to **Technoblade**, for inventing gravity. Thanks to all the **kids**. Thanks to **metal**. Thanks to **flowers** … JK! Thanks to **punk rock**. Thanks to **Corpse Husband** and thanks to **Skeppy**. Thanks to **Spifey**, one sexy mofo. Thanks to **Gogy**, keeping us all tough in times of need. Thanks to **Siri** for the dirty talk. Thanks to my **wall-jumping** ability that I was bestowed as a young man. How else would I climb? Thanks to **Cuba**.

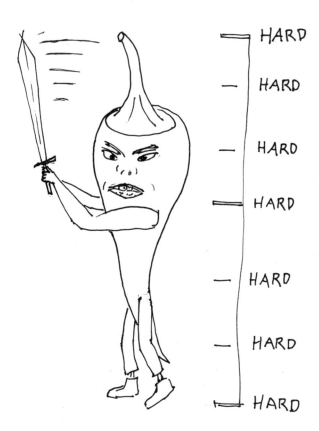

Okay, here's who we REALLY have to thank.

Thank you to the publishers, Quercus, for letting us put this in shops and stuff and making this silly little book real. They really shouldn't have. THANK YOU!

Thanks to Bognor, Elf and Amanda for helping us put this whole thing together.

Thanks to my dad. Not just for assisting in the birthing process, but for helping with the book also.

Thanks to my mum for telling me when to stop.

Thanks to Ash and Shelby and Cecily for helping us and listening to us tell the same joke over and over.

Thanks to Will's mum. For knowing the antidote.

Thanks to Philza Minecraft (obviously).

Thanks to Technoblade.

No, thanks to Tubbo.

And thanks to you lot for always watching, supporting, and just being real awesome.

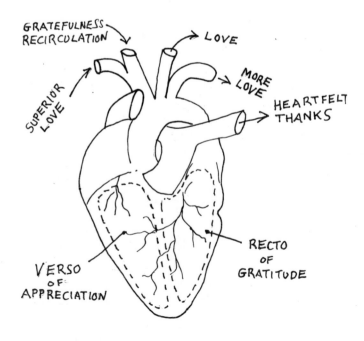